T0378752

OFF TO THE RACES

Mountain Bikes
Downhill

Thomas Kingsley Troupe

45TH PARALLEL PRESS

Published in the United States of America by Cherry Lake Publishing Group
Ann Arbor, Michigan
www.cherrylakepublishing.com

Reading Adviser: Beth Walker Gambro, MS, Ed., Reading Consultant, Yorkville, IL

PHOTOS CREDITS:
www.shutterstock.com, Cover ©Maciej Kopaniecki, page 2 ©Bagaskara Lazuardi, page 4 ©Jacek Chabraszewski, page 5 ©Kuznetcov_Konstantin, page 6-7 ©Maxim Petrichuk, page 7 ©Maciej Kopaniecki, page 8 ©Mauro Rodrigues, page 9 ©homydesign, page 10 ©michelangeloop, page 11 ©Kay Dropiewski, page 12 ©Wikichops (CCAS - https://creativecommons.org/licenses/by-sa/3.0/deed.en), page 13 ©bluedoor, page 14 ©Pierre Teyssot, page 15 ©homydesign, page 16 ©martin SC photo, page 17 ©Prostock-studio, page 18 ©Maciej Kopaniecki, page 19 ©Jean Francois Rivard| Dreamstime.com, page 20 ©federico neri, ©WUT.ANUNAI, page 21 ©Oleksandr Berezko, page 22-23 ©Gena73, page 24 ©Maxim Petrichuk, page 25 ©Grekov's, page 26 ©Jordi Mora, page 27 ©Maridav, page 27 ©12photography, page 28 ©Artem Oleshko, page 29 ©Lilkin, ©Dmitriy Kazitsyn, ©Dmitriy Kazitsyn, page 30©Africa Studio, page 31 ©Drazen Zigic, page 31 ©shutterstock.com art_Kelvin Degree

Produced for Cherry Lake Publishing by bluedooreducation.com

Copyright © 2026 by Cherry Lake Publishing Group

All rights reserved. No part of this book may be reproduced or utilized in any form or by any means without written permission from the publisher.

45th Parallel Press is an imprint of Cherry Lake Publishing Group.

Library of Congress Cataloging-in-Publication Data has been filed and is available at catalog.loc.gov.
Printed in the United States of America

Note from Publisher: Websites change regularly, and their future contents are outside of our control. Supervise children when conducting any recommended online searches for extended learning opportunities.

ABOUT THE AUTHOR

Thomas Kingsley Troupe is the author of over 300 books for young readers. When he's not writing, he enjoys reading, playing video games, and hunting ghosts as part of the Twin Cities Paranormal Society. Otherwise, he's probably taking a nap or something. TKT lives in Woodbury, MN, with his two sons.

Table of Contents

CHAPTER 1
Introduction... 4

CHAPTER 2
What's My Time?...12

CHAPTER 3
Crash and Burn..18

CHAPTER 4
The Gear 22

Let's Get Started! 30
Find Out More.. 32
Glossary 32
Index.. 32

Chapter 1
Introduction

Mountain bikes were invented around 50 years ago. They are rugged. They can ride on rough ground like rocks and bumps. Some riders wanted a mountain bike sport. They wanted to compete. Riders hoped to try something new. They wanted a challenge.

The first downhill speed race was in 1976. It was called the Repack Downhill. It was held in Marin County, California. Riders would race down a steep hill. Mud, rocks, and tree roots made the races exciting.

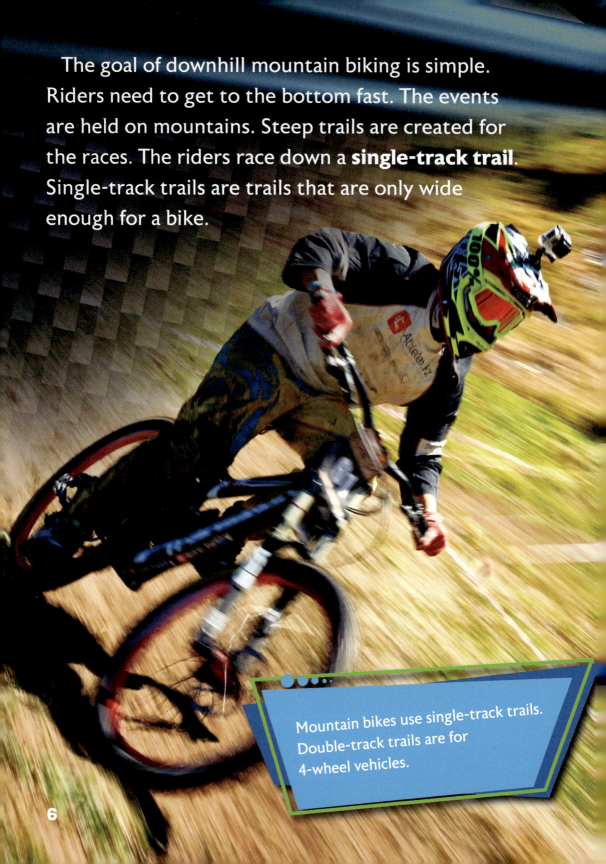

The goal of downhill mountain biking is simple. Riders need to get to the bottom fast. The events are held on mountains. Steep trails are created for the races. The riders race down a **single-track trail**. Single-track trails are trails that are only wide enough for a bike.

Mountain bikes use single-track trails. Double-track trails are for 4-wheel vehicles.

Downhill mountain bike racing is a **gravity** sport. Gravity is the force that pulls things to Earth. It pulls the bike down the mountain. Riders barely need to pedal. The steep trails give them speed.

The trails are difficult. Steep drop-offs create dangerous rides. Bumps can send bikes into the air. Sharp turns demand quick reflexes. It takes skill to stay on 2 wheels. Riders need to ride fast and safe.

This rider gets prepared for air time.

Riders stand for most of the race. They need strong arms and legs. Landing jumps is tricky. Good balance keeps riders from falling.

It helps to be prepared! Downhill mountain bike racers scout the course. They do a course walk before the race. They will see the **obstacles** along the trail. Obstacles are things in the way. Riders plan the best route downhill.

Weather can change a course. Rain and snow can create challenges. This can make the race harder.

The course walk can be a tough hike uphill. Riders can test-ride the course too. This lets them practice. It helps them find a safe and fast line downhill.

Chapter 2
What's My Time?

Downhill mountain bike races are timed. Their time starts at the top. It ends at the bottom. Riders want to know how fast they finished. The best time determines who wins. Skilled and brave riders win races.

The race begins at the top in what is known as the starting gate. It's up to the riders to speed to the finish.

Mammoth Mountain in California has an old ski hill. It was nicknamed "Kamikaze." One of the first downhill mountain bike races was held there in 1985. The trail is over 3 miles (5 kilometers) long. Riders can reach speeds of over 60 miles (96 km) per hour!

Digital laser timers are used in the races. One is placed at the starting gate. The other waits at the finish line. When a rider crosses the starting gate laser, the time starts. The rider races down the course. The rider crosses the finish line laser. This stops the timer.

Riders do whatever they can for the best time. Some runs are very fast. Many only last a few minutes.

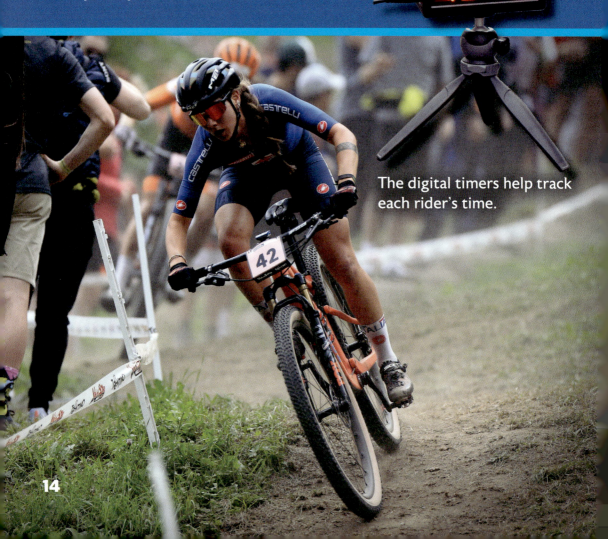

The digital timers help track each rider's time.

The rider with the best time wins points, cash, and prizes.

Downhill races are held in many countries. Racer number 204 crosses the finish line at a race in Portugal.

Some racers compete and race on a **circuit**. Circuit racing means competing in a series of races. In circuit races, riders have to earn leader points. These are points from each race. The most points are earned by winning each race on the circuit.

Winners of a mountain bike downhill race in France

16

When the last race in the circuit is finished, all the points are counted. The rider with the most points wins.

There are local and state events. Most riders start there. There are national organizations too. They sponsor downhill racing events. A large organization is USA Cycling. It developed the Downhill National Series. USA Cycling events take place all over the United States.

States with mountains have the most downhill mountain bike events. Vermont, Utah, North Carolina, and California all have large mountains. Their steep trails make the races challenging and exciting!

Chapter 3

Crash and Burn

Crash and burn means a rider has fallen. They are no longer in the race. Crashing on a bike is no fun. Falling on rough ground hurts! Serious injuries can happen. A fast, downhill fall can be disastrous.

OUCH! Racing a bike down a mountain can be painfull.

Riders need to be skilled and fearless. Bike crashes happen all of the time. A good rider knows that and competes anyway. The trails are designed to be challenging. If runs are too easy, the races lose excitement.

Professional downhill riders don't race to crash. They race to win.

Injuries happen. Races have medical crews standing by. They can get to the fallen rider quickly. First aid can be given right away.

There is always medical staff available at every race.

Riders are not the only ones to get hurt. Mountain bike damage happens too. A ruined bike means the rider's race is over. Some bikes can be repaired. Others need to be replaced. Mountain bikes are expensive. A professional racing bike costs thousands of dollars.

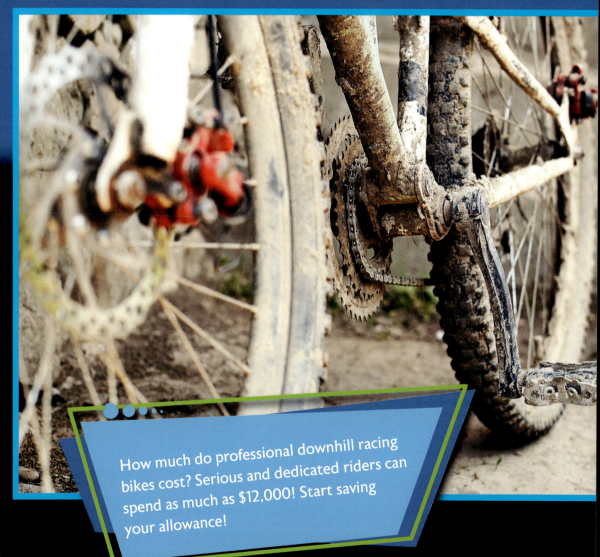

How much do professional downhill racing bikes cost? Serious and dedicated riders can spend as much as $12,000! Start saving your allowance!

Chapter 4
The Gear

Downhill bikes are built for speed. They have heavy-duty brakes. The bike's high-end frame is made from lightweight metal or **carbon fiber**. Carbon fiber is a lightweight man-made, material. The **suspension**, or shocks, helps the bike absorb impact and ride over bumps.

racing seat

knobby tires

rear suspension

heavy-duty disc brakes

cleated pedals

There are many different bikes to choose from. You can upgrade them with custom parts.

rubber hand grips

heavy-duty brake handles

front suspension forks

front disc brakes

Downhill mountain bike racers wear special gear. The gear helps keep the rider safe.

- full face helmet
- goggles or glasses
- shoulder pads
- elbow and forearm pads
- chest plate
- padded gloves
- knee and shin guards
- shoes with grip

Racers prepare like other athletes. They train in the gym to build strength. They spend countless hours on their bikes and trails.

25

Equipment Maintenance

An important part of mountain bike riding is **maintenance**. It means keeping something working and in good shape. Bikes and body armor can get damaged riding downhill. Checking and fixing the bike and gear often is smart. It keeps riders safe and bikes running smoothly.

Bikes get filthy after a race. It is smart to clean them up before the next one!

Riders can find mechanics at bike shops. Mechanics can do repairs. They can help keep the bike trail-ready. What happens if a racer's ride is damaged far from a shop? Most riders can do their own repairs. It can help save a race or training ride!

Portable bike repair multitool

Serious mountain bike riders fix their own bikes when possible. Doing repairs themselves saves time and money.

It's important to have the right tools. Ready-made bike repair tool kits are useful. They have both basic and specific bike tools.

A spare **tire tube** is good to have too. A tire tube is the inside of a bike tire. It keeps air trapped. A flat tire gets riders nowhere fast!

A bike repair tool kit

Flat tires are very common. Most riders keep a spare tire tube and air pump with them.

Let's Get Started!

Do Your Research

- Don't buy a bike just by reading ratings and reviews.
- Ask a bike store professional questions. Be honest about your mountain bike skills.
- Do not spend too much money on your first bike. You can find a good, affordable ride. The same goes for safety gear. Just don't ride without it!
- Find a local mountain bike club. Find a partner to ride with you.
- Take it easy! Practice balance and braking. Do not rush to a steep hill right away.
- Have a plan. Always let someone who is not with you know when you are biking the trails, and which trails you will be on.

Get In Shape

Lift weights to build strength.

Single-leg stand to build balance.

Jump rope or run to build cardio.

Stretch to build flexibility.

Find Out More

BOOKS

Abdo, Kenny. *Mountain Bikes.* Minneapolis, MN: Abdo Publishing, 2018.

Turnbull, Stephanie. *Mountain Biking.* Mankato, MN: Black Rabbit Books, 2016.

WEBSITES

Search these online sources with an adult:

Mountain Biking | Kiddle

Mountain Bike Racing | National Geographic

Glossary

carbon fiber (KAHR-buhn FYE-bur) a man-made material used in manufacturing that is more flexible and stronger than metal

circuit (SUR-kit) a type of racing where each event is made up of a series of races

gravity (GRAV-ih-tee) the force that pulls things to the center of the Earth and keeps things from floating away

maintenance (MAYT-nuhnts) keeping something in good or working condition

obstacles (AHB-stuh-kuhlz) things in the way or things that make it hard to achieve something

single-track trail (SIN-guhl TRAK TRAYL) a path that is just wide enough for bikes only

suspension (suh-SPEN-shuhn) a part of a bike that absorbs impact and helps protect the rider from bumpy ground

tire tube (TYER TOOB) the hollow rubber ring inside a bicycle tire that is filled with air

Index

carbon fiber, 22
course, 10, 11, 14
crash(es), 18, 19, 24

downhill, 5-7, 15, 17, 19

gear, 22, 24, 26, 30

injuries, 18, 20

maintenance, 26

obstacles, 10, 24

safety, 30
suspension, 22
single-track, 6
strength, 25, 31

timer(s), 14
tools, 28
trail(s), 6-8, 10, 11, 17, 19, 22, 24, 25, 30
training, 27
tube(s), 28, 29

USA Cycling, 17